Bloo

CW01336944

Isabel Wright has a B.A. in Dr

Scottish Academy of Music and Drama. In 2001 she was the Writer in Residence at the Traverse Theatre and she was subsequently the 2002 Writer in Residence at the Bush Theatre. Her first play, *Speedrun*, opened at the Tron Theatre in Glasgow in 1998. Subsequent plays include: *Waiting Room* with Complete Productions in 2000, *Tongues* with LookOut Theatre Company in 2001, *Initiate* and *Blooded*, both for Boilerhouse also in 2001, *Peepshow* for Frantic Assembly, which opened at the Drum in Plymouth in September 2002 before going on a UK tour and opening at the Lyric Theatre, Hammersmith in November 2002, *Mr Placebo*, opened at the Traverse in February 2003, directed by Wilson Milam, and her translation of *15 Seconds* was also performed there in March 2003 in a production directed by Roxana Silbert. Her most recent play, *Gilt*, co-written with Stephen Greenhorn and Rona Munro for 7:84 Theatre Company, toured Scotland last year before coming to the Soho Theatre in November 2003. Isabel lives in Edinburgh and is currently under commission to the Traverse Theatre.

Capercaillie Books

Blooded

by Isabel Wright

CAPERCAILLIE BOOKS LIMITED

First published by Capercaillie Books Limited in 2005.

Registered Office 1 Rutland Court, Edinburgh.

Design by Ian Kirkwood Design.

Typeset by Chimera Creations in Cosmos and Veljovic.

Printed in Great Britain by Antony Rowe Ltd., Chippenham, Wiltshire.

A catalogue record for this book is available from the British Library.

ISBN 0-9549625-4-0

The publisher acknowledges support from the Scottish Arts Council towards the publication of this title.

'Blooded' was first performed by Boiler House Theatre Company, directed by Paul Pinson at the Byre Theatre, St. Andrews on 26 October 2000. It was subsequently produced by the National Theatre as part of the Shell Connections Scheme.

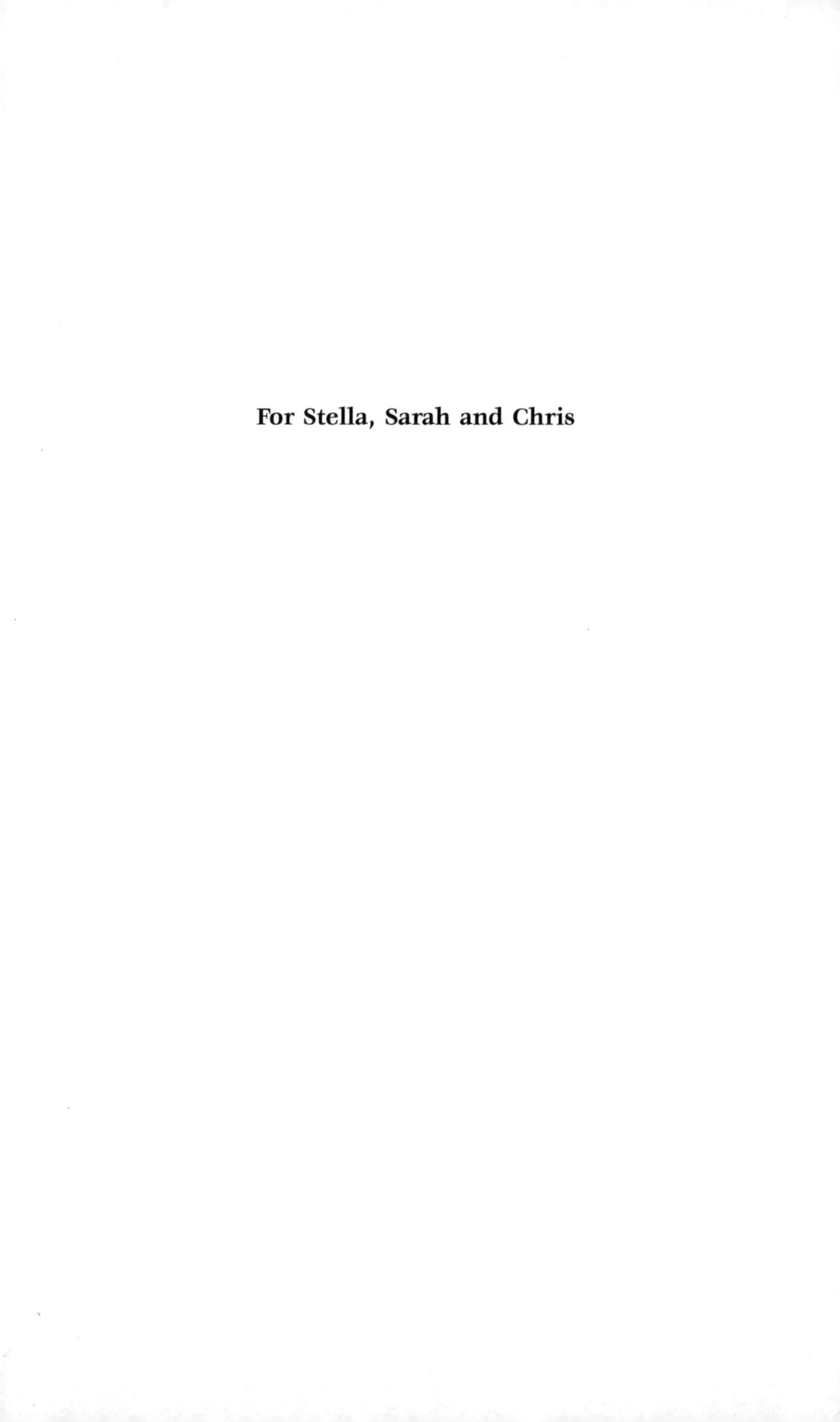

For Stella, Sarah and Chris

Introduction

Blooded was originally commissioned by Boilerhouse Theatre Company. I spoke to Artistic Director Paul Pinson about writing a play about a girl gang and he felt this was an idea his company could work with. I wrote the play drawing on a number of sources and experiences. I worked with Boilerhouse's Education Drama Worker in a few city youth centres discussing ideas with some of the young women there.

An important theme for the play came from talking to a young woman in a workshop who said that young women had to choose whether to be 'quiet' or 'a slag'. I found it very sad that after decades of feminism young women were still struggling with a sort of Mother/Whore range of choices. I wanted to explore how young women could find confidence and strength and in a way the characters all get this wrong. Amy thinks she has to be more aggressive than all the boys to be powerful, Donna thinks being sexually aggressive is the only way to make your mark.

Once I had an early draft I was able to workshop with some acting students from Queen Margaret college. I was then around 23 so I fed in cultural ideas and humour from my own viewpoint, and was also able to get feedback from the 19 year old students as well as the teenage youth centre participants. Although the play has quite specific cultural references I wanted it to have a fairly universal feel.

I found the process of writing *Blooded* far easier than some of my other commissions. I had a lot of fun once I found the voices of the girls, and the play's style came about instinctively. I wanted to find quite a lively physical way of writing which could go with the physical high energy that Boilerhouse theatre company are known for. I was interested in the way that groups of teenage girls you encounter on street corners have an incredibly powerful quality of seeming both terrifying and terrified at the same time. The makeup and clothes they often wear seem to make them look more sophisticated and more vulnerable at the same time.

In the background of the play are ideas to do with growing up in a society that constantly tells young women that a rapist is on the loose, and that violence is round the corner for them. Statistics seem to suggest that actually it is young men who are often more likely to be attacked on the street and yet as a young women you feel a tangible threat. The 'Dead Girl' comes to represent this fear, as well as symbolising various ideas to each of the young women. She terrifies Amy with the thought of mortality, Lou encounters the dark side with maturity, to FatB she is the impossibly perfect feminity that has always evaded her, to Donna she is weakness.

The plays charts the small tragedies that crack open the girls' childhood friendships as they head towards adulthood. The gang's cocky strength relies on a certain dynamic which allows the girls no room to change. Donna cannot handle it when FatB blossoms as she has always relied on FatB as her confidante and awestruck sidekick. Amy finds it difficult to accept Lou's criticism of her aggression. Tess' character symbolises the real tragedy of the play but we hopefully understand FatB's need to have her own life. Tess represents the kind of young person who is too prickly and intense to reach out to anyone, yet who is desperately lonely and needs someone to listen and understand.

I hope that readers will relate to these young women and their struggle to find their true selves. In striving so hard to be something they are not, they cannot seem to see where their own strengths really lie.

Isabel Wright, 2005

Characters

AMY:	teenager, 16.
DONNA:	teenager, 16.
LOU:	teenager, 16.
FATB:	teenager with weight problem, 16.
TESS:	FATB's younger sister, 14.
DEAD GIRL:	teenager.
VOICES:	various.

Setting

Town in Scotland.

Scene 1

The Dead Girl appears. She is sixteen, slim, pretty, with long blonde hair. She is dripping wet, covered in seaweed and strips of plastic and rubbish from the beach. She looks both grotesque and beautiful at the same time. A girl, FATB appears. She is sixteen.

FATB: She's under the curve of the Prom. A tattoo of sand gritted to her skin. She's blue and green and silver like a fish. I stop.

FATB and the Dead Girl look at each other.

FATB: All the blood in me freezes.

The Dead Girl smiles.

FATB: She's perfect so she is. A mermaid. I want to hold her till she's warm. Its not real. Its not happening. Its a film. Its Taggart. I want it to stop.

The Dead Girl disappears.

Scene 2

AMY, DONNA and LOU appear. They pace around the space in their own pattern of movement. Then, all together they stop.

AMY: We were all there that Summer.

LOU: Was a good Summer.

DONNA: Was a shite Summer.

LOU: No it wasn't!

AMY: Ay, it was.

LOU: So we were there that Summer.

AMY: Was an alright Summer.

DONNA: Bit of boozin' messin' about.

AMY: Waiting for something to happen.

LOU: Something to happen.

DONNA: Anything to happen.

The lights flash on, blinding white, AMY, LOU, DONNA and FATB break suddenly into a dance routine, like the slick routines in videos. They do this with various degrees of panache, but without self consciousness. The lights flash on again, blinding white, they freeze, then . . .

Scene 3

AMY has a can of beer. She chases about the space keeping it out of reach of DONNA, who crashes after her. FATB sits on the floor. LOU watches AMY and DONNA helplessly. AMY opens the can of beer and lets it fizz out of the can all over DONNA. DONNA screams and retaliates, grabbing a huge bag of crisps and stuffing them down AMY's neck, and grinding them in her hair. They struggle with each other, then AMY bores of it suddenly and breaks away.

DONNA: Ye bitch.

AMY: Askin fur it.

DONNA: No get a shag smellin like a tuckshop will I?

AMY: No get a shag anyway.

DONNA: You can talk.

AMY: Dinny have to fling it about do I?

DONNA: Shut yer face, ye wee boy-girl. Ye wee scruffter.

AMY: Shut yer own.

DONNA: You n whose army?

AMY: Take you any day Donna Delaney.

DONNA: I eat ye fur breakfast, Amy Matheson and ye ken it. An I spit ye out for break n all.

FATB: Ye've wasted the beer then?

AMY and DONNA look sheepish.

DONNA: Was fun, but, Bernie. Was fun.

FATB: Ay, always is.

AMY and DONNA look at each other and laugh, then tickle each other mercilessly until FATB and LOU are forced to drag them apart. Then AMY and DONNA turn on FATB and LOU till all are helpless on the ground, exhausted with laughter.

DONNA: Where we going then?

FATB: I'm skint.

DONNA: There's a surprise.

FATB: Canny help it!

LOU: Somewhere good this time.

DONNA: You think of it then.

AMY: Go watch the game?

DONNA: Ay, get tae fuck!

LOU: A film or something?

FATB: I'm skint!

DONNA: Youse are fuckin useless, you know that? A film? We're no wee lassies! Something good!

FATB: Something that's a laugh. N cheap.

DONNA: Ach, you're fuckin cheap.

LOU: We do loads of good stuff!

DONNA: Like what?

LOU: That's why folk always want to hang with us, eh? Cos of the stuff we do.

DONNA: I'd never hang about with any of that shower.

LOU: We're the best eh?

FATB: The best!

AMY: Know what we'll do?

DONNA: What?

AMY: Chum us to the hospital?

DONNA: Boring!

AMY: Chum us up the top the scaffoldin then?

DONNA: You fuckin wouldnae!

LOU: You can't!

AMY: Can't stop me.

DONNA: You'll no do it. You'll be peeing your pants at the sight of it.

LOU: You can't Amy!

AMY: Dare you then.

DONNA: Dare you back.

AMY: Dare you what?

DONNA: Fuckin name it.

AMY: You fuckin name it!

DONNA: Awright. Bet ye ma Gucci jeans you canny.

AMY: Don't fuckin want them!

DONNA: They're quality!

AMY: Nah, I'll do it for nothing,

AMY races off.

Scene 4

AMY is climbing the scaffolding. The others watch her climb.

DONNA: See us at the corner.

FATB: See us coming at you.

DONNA: N you see them take care.

FATB: N you see them take cover.

LOU: Cos we're something.

DONNA: Gonna be something.

FATB: Safe in the grip n the lock of what we've got.

DONNA: Safe in the smile and the shock of what they havnae.

LOU: Safe in the same old –

DONNA: Same old –

FATB: Mad –

DONNA: Crashing –

FATB: Days of –

LOU: Amy, Lou –

DONNA: Donna –

FATB: Bernie.

LOU: See us at the corner.

DONNA: See us coming at you.

FATB: An you see them take care

DONNA: An you see them take cover.

FATB: Cos they canny quite make it.

LOU: Cos they canny quite break us.

DONNA: Cos they'll never fuckin be us!

FATB: Hard as they try!

LOU: See us at the corner.

DONNA: There, looking skywards.

LOU: Watching Amy, Amy, Amy, reaching for the stars.

DONNA: Watching the mad bitch clinging to the bars.

FATB: Watching her climb for all of us, carry us on her back.

LOU: N she's there.

FATB: N she's made it!

LOU: N we breathe.

DONNA: Took yer time.

FATB: N she's there!

LOU: Tiny against the sky.

DONNA: Proving us wrong.

LOU: Makin it all right.

DONNA: Showing off.

FATB: Takin us –

LOU: Up, somewhere –

DONNA: On somewhere –

FATB: Wondering where we want to be.

LOU: Amy in the sky wi diamonds.

DONNA: Cocky cow.

FATB: Amy at the top. N us wi her.

AMY is on the top of the scaffolding by the hospital. She climbs onto the roof.

AMY: Into the world burst Amy followed by Lou, crashing an smashing at life and the world no a patch on us, into the world burst Amy, reaching up at the stars and almost almost takin them wi both hands. Into the heavens burst Amy, a mad girl and an eejit and a nippy wee bitch wi too much to say fur herself, but fighting fur Lou, and fighting fur the girls, and takin us all on whatever they say about us, cos we're made of steel us, an the bullets just bounce off us, and we're out stalking the town and the way folk smile and talk means nothing to us, cos we've been there always, ever since Lou first opened her gob to say 'you're my bestest pal in the world', ever since Amy first opened her gob and took on all comers, ever since Amy took her first steps and hit the world running, Cos you can see the whole world fae here, and there's no bedroom ceiling crushing down on you, an there's no disappointed faces at every turn, you're a queen here girl, and if you took off a step, the world'd catch you, the world'd fuckin catch ye and set you on its way! Cos if there is Amy, and there is Lou, and there is Donna and there is FatB! If there is all that! If there is – us! Us! Then fuck! The world'll stop and let us pass when we're coming at it, and one day you'll be heading out of this pokey wee mess o a town into something like a life, and there'll be no stopping you then Amy! There'll be no fuckin stopping you then! Hey! Hey Lou! Step out over the edge! And the world'll catch us Lou! The world'll fuckin catch us!

The sound of LOU screaming 'AMY!' Echoes round the space. LOU, DONNA and FATB are staring up at AMY. The Dead Girl appears. She passes alongside FATB, who turns and sees her. FATB freezes, they look at each other. The Dead Girl disappears.

Scene 5

DONNA, FATB, LOU and AMY are together. DONNÁ is staring at her face in a mirror looking for spots. AMY is kicking at things.

AMY: You know what sums the whole thing up?

LOU: What?

AMY: The little mermaid.

LOU: What?

AMY: That book we read when we were wee. I hate that fuckin book - it used to give me nightmares.

DONNA: I don't know it.

AMY: You do!

DONNA: I fucking don't!

AMY: Disney did it. With singing fish.

DONNA: Oh that thing.

AMY: You've got this mermaid girl right? An she cuts about the water cool as fuck. An then she meets this loser guy – he's a prince or something – isn't he a prince?

LOU: Probably.

AMY: An then cuttin about wi the seahorses isnae enough for her anymore. An she starts on and on and she's getting on the other mermaids' tits with her carryin on.

DONNA: I know the feelin –

AMY: An then the only way to be with him is to cut off her tail! An its really fuckin sore to walk about on her new legs but she does it cos she loves him, an its like the way my Mum hobbles about on crap high heels!

FATB: How is it?

DONNA: Don't knock heels!

LOU: Get old Imelda Marcos here –

DONNA: Who?

LOU: She had a lot of shoes.

AMY: All I'm sayin is –

DONNA: What the fuck are you saying?

AMY: The story sucks! An they shouldn't give it to kids!

FATB: The Disney one was allright –

AMY: The point is – ! What the fuck's it meant to teach us? To cut ourselves up for love? Marry a prince?!

DONNA: What the fuck's she on about?

FATB: Fuck knows.

LOU: Its just a story Amy, what's it matter?

AMY: My point exactly!

DONNA: Eh? **(Beat)** Hey, FatB! Tell us how you found her on the beach again!

LOU: You're a sicko, Donna.

DONNA: I know, but tell us!

FATB: No.

AMY: I think I saw him.

DONNA: When?!

AMY: I did! I walked home that night!

LOU: Amy!

AMY: Why not?

DONNA: You're such a fuckin mum Lou.

AMY: Boysey was pissing me off trying to cop a feel, an I hate feelin you have to stay with some arse rather than go where you want! An I wanted a walk! The night was magic!

DONNA: You never saw him!

AMY: I saw the car. White Mazda.

DONNA: You're no sure though.

AMY: Doin all this weird driving. Had to be him.

DONNA: You gonna tell the cops?

AMY: Tell em what? An nobody calls them cops Donna, fuck sake.

DONNA: My Dad calls em 'fashies'.

AMY: You what?

LOU: Like fascists.

AMY: Oh.

LOU: It could've been you, Amy!

AMY: Why can't I walk home if I want to? If I'm with some bore or some plukey wee boy tryin to stick his tongue in?

DONNA: Don't get stuck wi plukey boys then.

AMY: Why shouldn't I walk?

LOU: Cos you might end up dead.

DONNA: What were you doing on the beach that morning anyway?

FATB: Walkin Rizla

DONNA: That fat wee pug!

FATB: He's not fat!

DONNA: His skin's three sizes too big for him!

FATB: Leave Rizla out of it!

DONNA: Calm yoursel'.

Pause

FATB: Its her funeral soon.

LOU: Its a shame.

FATB: I'm gonna go.

DONNA: An I get called sick!

LOU: You never knew her B.

FATB: I found her! I sat with her! Called on my mobile and sat with her till they came!

LOU: What did you do?

FATB: When?

LOU: While you were waitin for them.

FATB: Nothin. Didn't touch her. Remembered that from the telly. Didn't cover her up or nothing. I wanted to! I wanted to cover her up!

DONNA: You just sat and looked at her!

FATB: She needed company. After everything.

DONNA: She's hardly gonna know you're there, is she?

FATB: How do you know? If that was me, and some bastard'd done that to me, and someone had found me lyin there, and they couldn't even look at me, and they left me all alone again . . . !

LOU: What if he'd come back?

FATB: He wouldn't have.

LOU: How d'you know?

FATB: They always crawl back into the woodwork.

DONNA: No gonna hang about to get caught.

FATB: Naw.

AMY: Naw.

DONNA: Naw.

Lights change.

AMY: See us at the corner.

DONNA: See us coming at them.

LOU: An you see them stand back.

AMY: An you see them take cover.

LOU: Cos we're strong.

DONNA: Cos we're something.

AMY: An they don't know what we've got.

DONNA: But they want it.

LOU: See us coming at them.

FATB: Scared of what we might do!

DONNA: Scared of what we might become!

FATB: See us!

AMY: An fear us!

DONNA: We can buy the world!

AMY: Crush it under foot!

LOU: Take hold of anything.

AMY: Take on the world and win.

LOU: An they know it!

DONNA: They can see it.

FATB: An you see them looking at each other.

AMY: You see em stop an wonder.

DONNA: When it happened.

LOU: Cos we were wee lassies.

AMY: 'They were such nice wee lassies'.

DONNA: And now we wipe em out with a look.

AMY: Slice through em.

DONNA: With a sneer or something.

FATB: We can be whatever the hell we want and they know it!

AMY: And they don't quite cut it.

LOU: They see us coming at them –

AMY: An they move out the way!

Scene 6

The light focuses in on AMY and LOU.

LOU: Into the world burst Amy, closely followed by Lou!

LOU: Since . . . forever . . . since . . . first day of nursery. Me and Amy met in the sandpit.

AMY: Doctor Lou. Our baby genius.

LOU: She was so cool.

AMY: A double act.

LOU: She had good bunches.

AMY: Dangerous.

LOU: Funky dungarees.

AMY: Flyin down the Prom on a shared pair o skates.

LOU: And this wee boy comes up and tries to muscle in. He's got a whiny wee voice, and no one's ever said no to him his whole four years of life.

AMY: Sling an arm round Lou.

LOU: Cos I'm hers and she's mine. She lets fly a look. Like . . .

AMY: This sandpit aint big enough for the two of us.

LOU: Wee gnaff doesn't get the hint. So she gives him the biggest shove, and he goes reelin reelin back, his arms flyin, and the look on his face! Then I knew what she was! Magic! And that was us.

AMY: Stuck together.

LOU: Like glue. Like cement. Like forever. Nothing gettin past us, eh Amy? Nothin in this world.

There is a flash of white light and LOU and AMY freeze, stuck in a pose as for a photobooth photo, then . . .

Scene 7

AMY is moving about, she has condoms blown up like balloons, is hitting them into the air. She grabs LOU round the neck and blows a raspberry into her ear, then hits a condom balloon to her.

LOU: Did you buy them?

AMY: Don't be daft! Old hackitface gave us them.

LOU: In class?

AMY: Told her I'd been shaggin away since I was ten. Could've been too, Donna has been . . . pretty much.

LOU: No she hasn't!

AMY: Well, whatever. Told her I was too skint to buy them and I'd go right home and get pregnant just to show her. Told her she shouldnae sit there with that moralising face on her. Told her she should just fuckin give us what we need to keep safe and say nothin. I said fuck n all!

LOU: You didn't!

AMY: I did!

LOU: But you don't even need them, Amy!

AMY: She doesn't know that! I'm your fear, I says! My great ambition is to have a baby and beat the council flat queue! They'll get the joke, I figured. They'll say, you're sharp, Amy, ironic. You can be a brain surgeon, a physicist, a UN ambassador like Geri Spice (you're fuckin jokin man!) But she thought I meant it. She says, 'You're capable of anything'. An I says, 'Ay, I am!' Just fuckin wait n see!

LOU: What'll they do to you?

AMY: Dunno. Big chat about 'my language and attitude in the classroom situation' I expect.

LOU: You're a nutter Amy!

AMY: Ay,ay, tell me something I don't know.

AMY starts to roll herself a cigarette.

LOU: Don't!

AMY: What?

LOU: What about your Dad?

AMY: Ach, he had a good old time before he went.

LOU snatches away the fag and crushes it with her shoe.

AMY: Hey, what're you doing?

LOU: I'm not watching you die!

AMY: Lou!

LOU: Lets get some chips.

AMY: Come on then.

Scene 8

Light comes up on DONNA. She is lifted onto someone's shoulders. The others gather around her, crushed together and laughing, pushed by the crowd and moving as if in slow motion.

DONNA: The Summer of T in the Park! An we get a tent and its muddy as fuck! An you wake up in the morning with inch thick mud on your face! An just when you think you've got through the day all clean some wee eejit comes and splashes your best white jeans or hugs you when he's muddy, just to be funny. An the food's all right, but its dead expensive man! Fuck me so it is! But when you're right there in the middle of it! An there's so many, many people and you've never seen that many people in your life all together! An the sun's going down and its rainin like fuck down on you likes! But you don't care cos its the best thing ever! An there's a big man on your right who's like a big fuckin wall! An there's a big man on your left who's like seven foot tall, and then there's a big wave when everyone gets swept right along and you're in the middle of it! And Amy canny stand up any more so you're draggin her to her feet. And some wee gnaff's tryin to snog you so you're fightin him off likes! An you've lost your sister long ago cos she had to stand up the back by the kebab van cos of the baby. But you can still see! And everyone's jumpin, jumpin, and you're jumpin, jumpin, and everyone carries you with them, and there's some big guy puts you on his shoulders and you're high above everyone reachin for the skies! An you're wavin at the camera an you might get on the telly! An its the best – the best – and one day it'll be you up there onstage with millions and millions of folk standin and wavin and thinkin you're it! An that'll be you made Donna Delaney! That'll be you made!

White lights come up bright like a stadium, and there is the sound of a huge crowd roaring. DONNA basks in the glory.

FATB: Don't even think of tellin her!

DONNA slides down from their shoulders with a bump.

DONNA: Tell us what he said!

LOU: Nothing.

DONNA: Tell us! You can't be feart! If Darren says something I want to hear it! To my face and not behind my back!

LOU: **(mumbles)** He says you were his friend.

DONNA: What?!

LOU: He was chatting up some girl and he says he's not had a girlfriend for a whole year and you were just his best friend.

DONNA: You're lyin to me!

LOU: I'm not! I'd never!

DONNA: I'll kill him!

LOU: He was all over her by the Slam tent.

DONNA: I'll tear him apart! An I'll tear her apart! Fuck! I loved him, Lou! I loved him! An its all a lie so it is! He's betrayed me! He's a fuckin Judas!

Scene 9

LOU: We were all there that Summer –

FATB: Scraping by –

AMY: An scrappin with each other –

FATB: Feelin like the world was closin in on us.

DONNA: Feelin like no one really heard what you were sayin –

LOU: Just this endless stream of words –

FATB: Like we were mad mouthin underwater.

AMY: Banging your fists against windows –

DONNA: Of the places you'd never get into.

AMY: Smashing a fist –

DONNA: Through the glass that stops you.

LOU: Trying.

FATB: Tryin.

LOU: Trying to be what they need you to be.

AMY: Pulled in all directions.

FATB: House too small –

AMY: An you too big.

FATB: Legs an arms sprawlin out through windows an doors. Stuck in a poky wee room, dreamin huge dreams.

LOU: We were all there that Summer. Amy and Lou.

DONNA: FatB and Donna.

FATB: An Tess.

DONNA: An Tess.

AMY: An Tess.

TESS appears. She is a fourteen year old Goth with braces, funny hair, DM boots and a tassle skirt.

TESS: I don't want to be fuckin Barbie or Buffy or Dawson or Lara Croft! I don't want to be Kylie or Geri or Kate fuckin twinset Winslet! Or Kate skinnyhips Moss! Or Zoe chirpy Ball! Or Skeleton Beckham! Or whatever fake girlpower riot girl they're shovin at us next! Not fuckin Steps! Or Weepy Gwynneth! Or Britney sparkly tits Spears! Or fuckin Louise!

Scene 10

AMY, LOU, FATB and DONNA. They are sprawled on the floor, arms round each other, playing with each other's hair, casual and comfortable in their physicality.

FATB: My Auntie's put me on another diet.

DONNA: Yeah?

AMY: Guess who I saw today?

LOU: Who?

FATB: I'll do it this time I reckon.

AMY: Scotya!

DONNA: What d'you get to eat?

LOU: Who the hell's that?

AMY: Primary Seven! You fancied him!

FATB: No carbohydrates. Just protein.

DONNA: You what?

LOU: No I never!

FATB: Its what Jennifer Aniston does.

DONNA: Are you sure?

AMY: You fuckin did!

FATB: Its true! You can have like chicken or fish or –

DONNA: No bread?

FATB: Nup.

LOU: Why would I have fancied him?

DONNA: No pasta?

FATB: Nup.

AMY: He had a cool wee gold ring –

DONNA: No.

AMY: An' his hair was all cute and curly at his neck!

FATB: You can have like . . . bacon . . . but no toast I guess. Or fish –

DONNA: But no chips?

AMY: An he was dead mouthy.

FATB: I s'pose.

LOU: You know a lot about it.

DONNA: Sounds like hell.

AMY: Maybe I fancied him.

FATB: Its a bit confusing.

AMY: Can't remember.

DONNA: Water's the way to do it.

LOU: That's more like it!

DONNA: Drink like twenty glasses a day.

FATB: I hate water.

DONNA: You don't hate it.

FATB: I do! I can't drink it!

AMY: Its awful that! You're so in love n that! You'd do anythin for them. Flunk something cos you're starin at them. Let em kiss you. Then six years later – you can't remember their name or nothin!

DONNA: Cucumber. Grapes. Lettuce. They've got nothin in them.

LOU: You remember his name?

FATB: N they taste of nothing n all.

AMY: Yeah, 'Scotya.

LOU: What kind of name is that?

AMY: He took stuff! 'Scotya purse! 'Scotya bag!

DONNA: Its just hard B.

LOU: That's really lame.

DONNA: Face that its hard.

AMY: I never made it up!

FATB: Thing is, right? I don't eat much.

DONNA: No?

LOU: Why's Spud called Spud?

AMY: Cos he looks like one?

LOU: That can't be it!

FATB: I eat less than Amy!

DONNA: She's always jumpin about.

AMY: He's got a Spuddy kind of face.

FATB: I eat less than Lou!

DONNA: Its how things are I guess.

FATB: It pisses me off.

LOU: He gets old and one day he runs into one of us and we're like, 'Spud! How're you doin man!' And then his wife and kids look at him and go, 'He does look like a Spud!' And then its all fucked.

DONNA: Maybe we're just meant to be like this.

FATB: You think I'm stuck being fat?

LOU: His kids are like – 'Fuck Dad, they called you Spud at school! An you said you were cool!'

DONNA: I never said you were fat.

FATB: You call me FatB!

DONNA: That's just a laugh!

LOU: FatB was dead funny last night. Dunny said something dead shan and she came right at him – she said – she said –

FATB: My Dad used to say I was bigboned.

DONNA: Yeah?

AMY: Never mind.

LOU: No – I'll – twas –

FATB: I don't think about it mostly. Its other people make you think about it. An you just feel sick.

DONNA: Don't think about it then. Maybe its like boys . . . my Mum says its when you're not trying to fall in love that it happens.

AMY: You never remember!

LOU: It was dead funny anyway. Fuck. I hate that.

FATB: What about if you're thinking about it but you're pretending not to be thinking about it?

AMY: I thought she fancied him.

LOU: FatB?

DONNA: I don't think that works.

FATB: Oh.

AMY: Why not?

LOU: Well . . . she's a laugh . . . she doesn't fancy anyone, does she?

Scene 11

The Dead Girl appears, dripping in water.

FATB: I can't sleep for seeing you. Mermaid girl. Everyone's got stories for what happened to you. What did he do to you?

The Dead Girl shakes her head.

FATB: What did he do?

The Dead Girl starts to circle FATB.

FATB: Did you see him coming at you? Did you know there was no way out?

The Dead Girl starts to look scared.

FATB: You had it all didn't you? Perfect. Skinny. Bet you were clever. Bet you were rich. Saw your Mum and Dad on the news. Looked like they had money. They looked terrible. Cried for you. Think people would cry for me?

The Dead Girl smiles and shrugs, then disappears. LOU DONNA and AMY appear.

FATB: Everyone keeps askin who'll be next.

LOU: We should be careful.

AMY: Fuck careful.

LOU: I clutch my keys when I walk home late from school.

DONNA: For what? So you can stab him with them?

LOU: Maybe.

AMY: Gives you a metal punch eh Lou? Get him in the balls.

DONNA: Stupid.

FATB: Dunny's brother's in the army. Took three guys out with a kebab!

DONNA: Shut up!

FATB: Three guys come at him and he just stays cool. Splits the kebab – pow – pow – blinds two of them. While they're stumblin round with kebab sauce in their eyes he takes out the middle one. Then he knocks their heads together, the two kebab boys. Three down, done and dusted.

AMY starts dancing round them as a boxer, the others are still laughing at FATB who is still acting out the kebab encounter.

AMY: I'm sick of bein afraid! I can outrun anyone! Stand ready! Maximum offence. Maximum defence. Punch like you mean it Mr Bailey says! Punch, punch-punch! Boys get in fights, cause trouble. We're the ones who get locked up. Get the flak. Its like your Mum always goin on about us not hangin round the amusements.

LOU: She doesn't like us hangin about there.

DONNA: Why not?

LOU: Cos that wee lassie –

AMY: Cos a wee lassie went missing there when we were six. But now why don't we hang about there?

LOU: People have long memories.

AMY: But we're old now!

LOU: Ghosts maybe.

DONNA: Why d'you want to go there anyway?

AMY: I don't.

DONNA: So what's yer fuckin point?

AMY: Youse never fight nothing! Youse just accept. You, **(To Lou)** letting all the teachers call you by your sister's name by mistake, and push you to do as well as her!

LOU: What's that got to do with –

AMY: Everything! Everything's got to do with everything!

DONNA: I don't get it.

AMY: Naw, you never do!

LOU, DONNA and FATB leave AMY on her own, sit down in the corner. DONNA pulls out a magazine. The Dead Girl appears to AMY. They face each other. Then AMY starts to get scared. She tries to move away from the Dead Girl. The Dead Girl follows her, then disappears. Light focuses on LOU.

LOU: The thing with Amy is – her head goes racing on without you. And just when you think you've got what she's thinking or who she likes she's off again. You can't catch her. Ever. And its always been.

VOICE 1: Amy's wild!

VOICE 2: And Lou's quiet.

VOICE 1: Lou's a good girl.

VOICE 2: Keep her on the straight and narrow.

LOU: But I don't want the straight and narrow! I want to go crashing off the track like Amy! I want the wild path off the edge of the computer screen!

VOICE 1: Lou'll do us proud.

LOU: But you should see Amy run! Flinging herself out to catch some ball! Saying all the wrong loud things that are somehow the right loud things! You love her! She's . . . your hero! She's all you can believe in sometimes!

AMY appears in a pool of golden light. Then she gives a scream of frustration.

AMY: Fuckhead comes – tries to squash me – to make me small. Fuckhead comes, with his baldy head and hair combed over. The world's so big and I want to tell him. The world's so full of things I want to do! 'What is it you want to achieve in life?' he says. I want to climb mountains, be a fighter, run races, charge down streets with bulls, bungee jump off the side of the world! I want to learn a million languages and make all the Fuckheads in the world understand me. I want to put them all together and smash a big brick into their fathead faces, make them do something with the world! I want to be more than a mouthy cow! More than –

VOICE 1: Amy has a degree of intelligence –

AMY: I want to take on the world and leave it shaking behind me! But I don't say all this! And Fuckhead comes with his sad wee vest showing through his shirt and says 'You'll have nothing, my girl, unless you BUCKLE DOWN! BUCKLE DOWN' he says, 'BUCKLE DOWN!'

The words 'Buckle Down' echo round the space as does AMY's laugh as she jumps down to join LOU. DONNA is reading a magazine, FATB joins her.

LOU: Why'd you do it?

AMY: Had no choice.

LOU: You can choose what you say.

FATB: What are you reading?

AMY: No I can't!

DONNA: The way you shave your legs and how it reveals your personality.

FATB: You what?

AMY: He was being a fuckhead and I couldn't stop myself!

DONNA: That's what it says!

LOU: Amy . . .

FATB: How many ways are there?

AMY: He needs to know! If I was a crumbly old fuckhead I'd want to be told!

DONNA: Loads.

LOU: He knows what you think of him.

AMY: He should!

DONNA: How often you do it.

AMY: He should know that someone he's supposed to teach thinks he's a loser.

DONNA: Whether you start at the shins.

LOU: Sometimes you have to learn to live with fuckheads.

AMY: He doesn't know what he is!

DONNA: Whether you only go up to your knees.

AMY: I mean, psychos don't think they're bad do they?

DONNA: Bikini line.

AMY: As far as they're concerned its cool killing people, an just a wee matter between them and the victim and the rest of the world shouldn't get involved.

DONNA: Brazilian – what's that?

LOU: Amy –

FATB: Please stop –

AMY: And Hitler never knew he was wrong!

LOU: What are you?

AMY: I know its different! I'm just saying, fuckheads should be told! Even if they're just little fuckheads, not Hitler or anything. I mean, if no one tells them then –

DONNA: Apparently I'm . . .

LOU: He probably knows he's a fuckhead Amy. That's the thing.

DONNA: Vivacious and ambitious with a strong feminine side.

LOU: Fuckhead must be, what, forty? If someone's that old it's too late to change. They don't need you rubbing their face in it.

DONNA: D'you think I am?

AMY: You always have to stick up for everyone.

LOU: No, I don't!

DONNA: Here. Numerology.

AMY: You do! You can't just hate someone can you? You have to find some way of letting them off the hook! You can't sit on the fence your whole life Lou!

DONNA: You have to add up your birthday, then add other stuff- and I'm a nine!

AMY: Nothing gets done! I sorted him out all right? And all the veins in his neck are standing out and I think he'll have a heart attack or something!

DONNA: That's intuitive and romantic, see!

AMY: Cos he knows he's a dinosaur and the future's me!

DONNA: You add up like a 5 and a 3 and a 1 and 9 –

AMY: We'll not grind them in the dust or nothing, the dinosaurs.

DONNA: And 8 and 3 and that's 2 –

AMY: But they'll not be patting us on the head like children anymore!

DONNA: And then you add 6 –

AMY: Cos we'll be taking control,

DONNA: And that's – oh,that's eight

AMY: Stealing it piece by piece!

FATB: It helps with your maths anyway.

DONNA: Is that your phone?

AMY: What?

DONNA: It's your phone.

AMY: It's not – it's your phone

DONNA: Is it your phone?

FATB: No

LOU: Don't look at me!

FATB: It's not my phone!

DONNA: It's somebody's phone!

AMY: There's no fuckin phone ringing Donna!

DONNA: There is! Amy, Lou. There's not!

A beat's silence while they listen for the imaginary mobile phone sound, then stalk away from each other in a sulk. The Dead Girl appears. She is sobbing. She is bruised. She stumbles through the space.

Scene 12

DONNA is in her shoeshop workshirt. She is applying lipstick.

FATB: You shouldn't be working all the time, its not good for you

DONNA: You can talk!

FATB: That's different. That's family.

DONNA: I'm good at it.

FATB: I know.

DONNA I'm shite at school.

FATB: You're not!

DONNA: Its ok. I know how things are. I know how to make the guys want me and the woman want what I sell.

FATB: Is that what you do?

DONNA: Course, I could make it to the top maybe. If that – that –

FATB: Arse?

DONNA: Yeah, if he'd move on.

FATB: Maybe we could like . . . tell his wife what he's like.

DONNA: She knows.

FATB: You reckon?

DONNA: She's divorcing him. He asked if I'd ever had 'a relationship crumble around me'.

FATB: You what?

DONNA: So I says, ay, I suppose I have.

FATB: Meaning Darren?

DONNA: Yeah, and he says, 'that is a babygrief compared to mine'.

FATB: What the fuck's that mean?

DONNA: He's always sliding up against me when he can behind the desk.

FATB: Eurgghh!

DONNA: Makes me run over to catch the bank before it closes and watches my tits bounce up and down like they do.

FATB: I hate that.

DONNA: His skin's all shiny like a cheese sandwich on a hot bus.

FATB: What a mingher!

DONNA: He wears the best stuff in the shop and makes it look sad.

FATB: I know. It sort of hangs funny off him.

DONNA: An he thinks I want him. Thinks I sit at that cash desk dreaming of rubbing against him – fondling his Disney ties.

FATB: You're making me sick!

DONNA: I'll end up his boss. That's what he knows.

FATB: Couple of years and you can sack him!

DONNA: I know how to play him. I know how to play all of them. Its how you get on, B, its what you have to do.

FATB: I'm rubbish at all that.

DONNA: I'll sort you out, you'll see. A bit of hairputty and some attitude and you'll be fine. Get that job at H & M. Anything.

FATB: You reckon?

DONNA: Just leave it to me. I'm your pal and I can get discounts.

FATB: You're brilliant Donna.

DONNA: You just need to say fuck off to your Da and sister is all.

FATB: Why?

DONNA: They hold you back, family.

FATB: Well . . .

DONNA: That's the answer B, you know it is.

Scene 13

TESS: One day it'll come up on the screen the answer you've been looking for. The reason why nothing seems real. And till it comes all you can do is bang your head against some majorvector A.I. wall and scream for help. Cos it aint coming in the shape of Amy, and it aint coming in the shape of Lou. It's gonna be bigger than Bernie could handle. Amy says she's free but she knows jackshit.com about freedom. Its gonna be bigger than they can imagine. Bigger than some kid finding out how to make bombs on the Net. It'll be minds falling down webrings, sliding down links into stuff they could hardly imagine. Its calling into the darkness to find a whole colony of mutants just like you. A whole new Zion calling you to it. And there's nothing they can do to stop us. Nothing.

Scene 14

AMY, LOU, DONNA and FATB. DONNA is absentmindedly walking through a dance routine she is making up, humming a tune away to herself. AMY is hanging from a part of the set. She jumps down and picks up LOU, slings her over her shoulder and swings her round, LOU giggles and AMY lets her down. FATB is daydreaming. AMY goes to DONNA and starts to get in the way of her dance steps, standing in front of her, trying to hook her legs out from under her, and tickle her waist. DONNA refuses to rise to the bait this time and calmly gets out of her way.

AMY: They're so fucking scared. Like we're some kind of sponges or something. Like any old bullshit folk tell us we're gonna take for the word of God. So its like, give a girl a c-card and make her a slag. Naw. Give Spud a condom and he'd never know what to do.

DONNA: There'd be no one for him to do.

FATB: You hear about Spud in Maths today?

DONNA: What did he do this time?

FATB: They all dared him to ask Sweetface McKenzie what masturbate meant.

DONNA: Did he do it?

FATB: You bet.

DONNA: Sad wee Spud.

AMY: What did McKenzie say?

FATB: Sweetface tells him in his ear and Spud gets a massive beamer and Sweetface turns to the class and says 'Its people like you that got Captain Pugwash banned'.

DONNA: **(losing her rag finally and shoving AMY out of her way)** What the fuck's that supposed to mean?

FATB: Fuck knows.

DONNA: I've gone off Sweetface. He's not that cute.

FATB: He is!

DONNA: And he says loads of weird stuff. That makes you think he just looks young and he's really dead old.

FATB: Like what?

LOU: Like going on about TV programmes that were on in the Ark.

FATB: He can't help that, can he? Its better than pretending he likes something just to impress us.

DONNA: You lurrve him! You lurrvve him!

AMY: Its a fucking mess this world.

LOU: What do you mean?

AMY: Sometimes I get this fear right? That one day we'll wake up all old and just as bad as the losers we slag off now. And we'll know there were all these times we could have done something to change things and we never. An we'll spend our days moaning about sex being boring, and not finding the right blinds for our windows, and we'll spend our nights shagging in front of *Who wants to be a millionaire* answering questions as we come, saying 'We love Ally McBeal' she knows how we feel!

DONNA: Lets never get old!

AMY: Lets never get braindead!

LOU: Lets never have dinner parties!

DONNA: Or spend our Saturdays in Ikea!

AMY: Lets never say, we should have changed the world, but there was never enough time!

TESS appears.

FATB: Hey Tess, you all right?

TESS: I guess.

DONNA: What're you creeping about for? Gave me a heart attack.

TESS: What're you talking about?

DONNA: Nothing.

AMY: Getting old.

TESS: What's wrong with getting old?

AMY: We're going to do something with our lives.

TESS: I guess everyone says that at our age. **(Pause)** What's for tea, B?

DONNA: **(mimicking her)** What's for tea, B?

FATB: Don't know yet. You hungry?

TESS: Starving.

DONNA stands behind TESS and impersonates her, FATB almost laughs despite herself. The others laugh also. The mood is ugly.

FATB: Can I . . . ? I'll just be . . . Give me twenty minutes eh?

TESS: Whatever.

TESS leaves.

AMY: Headcase! We'll be different, you'll see! We'll say we'll do stuff and then we'll do it!

LOU: It's ok, Amy.

AMY: Fuckin weirdo.

LOU: She's all right.

AMY: You think it too! At least I say it out loud!

LOU: How did it go today?

AMY shrugs.

LOU: What happened? What're they going to do to you?

AMY: They want me out.

LOU: They never said that.

AMY: They don't have to.

LOU: They can't kick you out.

AMY: They said I'm not going to pass anythin the way I'm goin so what's the point? Its my decision they said. But I've been warned.

LOU: You have to stay.

AMY: What's the point? Once they've started 'persuading' you out. Stamp failure on your forehead.

LOU: You'll do it.

AMY: What do you know? You never fail nothing! I can be smart sometimes I guess. At least I tell myself . . . I'm a different kind of smart, a kind they don't get. But I go in the exams an I panic. All goes to goo inside my head.

LOU: They brand me too. Keep on and on about what I should do.

AMY: Its not the same.

LOU: It is!

AMY: Its not! We're different now! I'm nothing! We do all this talkin-like all we need is you an me an fuck the rest! But you know what the world's sayin to me? We want nothin from you's what. From you, Amy, we want nothing!

Pause. LOU gets something from her pocket.

LOU: Here. It's for you.

AMY: What is it?

LOU: A friendship band. Look, I've got one.

AMY: Cool! Tie it on me.

LOU ties it on, they put their wrists together.

AMY: Blood brothers!

LOU: We'll be all right, Amy, I promise.

AMY: Yeah.

Scene 15

FATB: I'm the last one standing. Get folk home. I'm the one they know is there when they're fucking out of their tree. FatB'll be there. Big boobs B. Fat Momma. She'll get you up the road. Carry you to your door. Carrying this fatsuit round all day. I'm just a dog or something. A wee fat pet they keep around. If I wasn't funny I'd be nothing. 'Hey fatpet' I hear them.

VOICE: Hey B! Hey!

FATB: Its all around.

VOICE 1: Rolly-polly-big-jobby-rollo!

VOICE 2: Hey fat girl!

FATB: Its what I am.

VOICE 1: Fat girl!

FATB: No face. No brain.

VOICE 2: FATB!

FATB: Just fat. And my auntie says –

VOICE 1: Your face is quite pretty.

FATB: An my auntie says –

VOICE 1: If you'd use a bit of slap.

FATB: An my Dad used to say –

VOICE 2: Don't start her caking it on! Mutton dressed as lamb –

VOICE 1: Fatpig dressed as –

FATB: There's always another girl following me. Skinny. Pretty. I see her in my head. **(The Dead Girl appears.)** She fits in. Could've been me. Daughter they should have had. Pretty big sister they should have had. Pretty wee pal they should have had. Can't be me now. I ate and ate an killed her. **(The Dead**

Girl exits.) An my auntie says –

VOICE 1: People warm to her.

FATB: Like I'm a funny fat hot water bottle. An my Da used to say –

VOICE 2: She's always got a joke in her.

FATB: Food keeps chasing you all day. Its all you can think of. An I never eat the way they do.

Scene 16

LOU appears. She is starting to dress the way AMY dresses.

LOU: All I want is for Amy to see me . . . really see me . . . notice I'm there. When she hurts I feel it. When she laughs I'm on top of the world. But she's so busy taking on all comers. She hardly knows you're alive.

AMY comes flying into the space.

AMY: Always had this thing like I should've been a boy. Let my Dad down. Used to play footie with him, in my white patent leather T bar shoes.

LOU: She just goes flying past you –

AMY: I have a big mouth in class and my Mum says –

VOICE 1: Watch they don't call you bossy –

VOICE 2: Or strident –

VOICE 1: Or Thatcher –

AMY: Or something.

LOU: Everything she does – the way she flicks her hair, or blows smoke rings, the way she sits in a chair –

AMY: And I think of the boy I should've been.

LOU: Is just cool.

AMY: And those rugby boys we grew up next to. We wait patiently in class for them to spit some half baked sentence out! And everyone listens to them!

LOU: She knows her place in the world!

AMY: They never get called mouthy.

LOU: Her voice low – like too many late nights and fags –

AMY: An my Mum says –

VOICE 1: Feminist.

AMY: Is a dirty word that'll –

VOICE 2: Get you nowhere but sent to Coventry.

LOU: She was born knowing where she fits I guess.

AMY: And my Mum says to wear heels cos its –

VOICE 1: Playing their game.

LOU: She always fits whatever she does.

AMY: But I only like being quick and sleek on the footie pitch, and screaming at the top of my lungs, and running like a maniac, that's when I know who I am.

LOU: She always just fits.

AMY: That's when I feel at home.

LOU: She's always just . . . perfect.

AMY: I can shoot pool and shoot the breeze! Talk shit with the best of them! All these stupit girls around me – wee Britney types at school – silly wee skirts and wonderbras pushed up to here! Line them up against the dinner hall and – **(Makes a machine gun noise. Beat.)** But sometimes you feel you're getting it wrong – the battle. You talk like a guy, and run like a guy, but sometimes, inside you, you wonder if you're missing something.

Light changes.

LOU: Here, Amy, here!

AMY: What's up?

LOU: I got something for you! **(Pulls out a locket.)**

AMY: Why? Its not my birthday or nothing.

LOU: Put it on! Look, it opens! You can put a photo in it.

AMY: Oh . . . thanks.

LOU gives her the locket.

LOU: Its just for . . . it was you that's all.

AMY: I can't Lou.

LOU: You have to! Please!

AMY: You shouldn't give me stuff.

LOU: I want to.

AMY: Well . . . thanks . . . Its pretty.

AMY hugs LOU.

Scene 17

DONNA and FATB rush into the space.

FATB: Where did you do it then?

DONNA: Where d'you think?

FATB: At his house? Were his parents in?

DONNA laughs.

DONNA: Imagine them walking in on you!

FATB: So . . . was it any good?

DONNA: Takes years to get good.

FATB: Yeah?

DONNA: Unless you're a natural . . . like me!

FATB: So? Tell me!

DONNA: Tell you what?

FATB: Tell me all about it!

DONNA: Nothing to tell.

FATB: He won't put it like that. He'll tell everyone.

DONNA: You think?

FATB: Everyone'll say they knew.

DONNA: Everyone'll say they did it with me too!

FATB: So you're glad? You don't regret it?

DONNA: I don't regret anything I do!

FATB: Course.

DONNA: Chocolate is better. My Mum was right.

FATB: No!

DONNA: It's so hit and miss. A good cream egg you can depend on.

FATB: Think he will tell everyone?

DONNA: Who cares? Who cares what they think! You're a slag or you're quiet, that's what they all say. You're a girl to have tea with their Mum, or you're a girl for sex. An havin tea's boring! Who cares? What are boys anyway? Load of bighead bufties!

FATB: Ratpack o hassle!

DONNA: One track mind!

FATB: Getting your tights down!

DONNA: Can't live with them!

FATB: Can't live without them!

DONNA: Bunch of knobs!

Scene 18

DONNA: They start on at you again.

VOICE: How old were you?

VOICE 2: When did you lose it?

DONNA: On and on at you. And the whole world's had sex. And the whole world did it years ago. And you're the last one in the world so you are. And they did it . . . in a car or . . .

VOICE 2: In the square.

VOICE 1: On the cold hard gravel.

VOICE 2: Under coats at a party.

VOICE 1: In my Mum and Dad's bed.

DONNA: An some days you figure you're too square to show your face. So you talk the talk, like you've done it all too. An before you know it you've got a name.

VOICE 1: Slag.

DONNA: But who gives a fuck. Its better than being a –

VOICE 2: Virgin!

DONNA: Every time I open my mouth I'm sure they'll find out.

VOICE 1: Virgin!

DONNA: And they all believe me, FatB, Amy, Lou, all of them. And they're jealous.

VOICE 2: Virgin!

DONNA: Sometimes I want some different kind of story.

VOICE: A car!

VOICE 2: A bush!

VOICE 1: My Mum and Dad's bed!

DONNA: An I'll go so far with some boy, and then I'll know I don't love him enough. He's just a wee boy fumbling around. You're worth more than some crap wee lie. He's not the one to be all open and scared with. He's not the one to go there with. He never is.

The Dead Girl appears silently behind DONNA as she nears the end of her speech. DONNA looks her in the eye and tries to take her on. The Dead Girl isn't frightened of DONNA. It is DONNA in the end who backs off. The Dead Girl exits. DONNA is alone. She starts to go through her dance routine steps, she starts slowly, then gets faster and more frenetic, trying to work out her feelings through the

steps. Then she stops. FATB, LOU and AMY appear.

FATB: They found her clothes, you know that? He dumped them in a skip.

LOU: Do we have to talk about this again?

AMY: You afraid?

LOU: It gives me the creeps.

AMY: I'd have fought him off.

FATB: How can you say that? You think she never tried?

AMY: The police did a drawing of what they think he looked like.

FATB: He looked like a monster.

DONNA: Eyes like . . . holes . . .

LOU: He probably doesn't look like that.

DONNA: What d'you mean?

LOU: He probably looks normal. We probably know him!

DONNA: Shut up!

FATB: They've got everyone out looking for clues.

DONNA: What're they gonna find?

FATB: They can do stuff with tiny bits of fabric now, with hair, or skin or –

DONNA: You watch too much fuckin *Cracker.*

FATB: Its what I want to do when I'm older.

LOU: Thought you wanted to be a marine biologist?

DONNA: That was last week.

FATB: Stop taking the piss!

AMY: They interviewed my uncle.

DONNA: What?

AMY: He's got the right kind of car.

DONNA: What happened?

AMY: He was with my auntie and half the bowling club that night.

DONNA: Oh. **(Beat)** Imagine if it had been your uncle!

AMY: What?

DONNA: Well . . . it'd be mad . . . exciting!

AMY: Fuck off, Donna!

DONNA: It'd be crap for you, I know.

AMY: You're unreal.

FATB: They have to find him. They have to.

LOU: I'm scared.

AMY: Why? There's always a rapist on the loose. What're we gonna do? Never go out? Never live our lives? Its a load of balls.

Lights change.

AMY: There's a moment where you know –

LOU: Where you can feel –

AMY: Yourself get old.

DONNA: There's a moment where you can feel –

FATB: You've passed a line.

LOU: And you can be one of them, one of the adults, one of the living –

AMY: And you know you'll be one of them, one of the adults, one of the braindead –

FATB: And you're scared –

LOU: And you smile –

DONNA: And you want to run back –

AMY: And you want to chase on.

FATB: There's a moment where you know –

DONNA: You're not a kid anymore –

AMY: And they'll keep trying to push you about –

DONNA: Mess you about –

AMY: Fuck you about.

FATB: But they'll see it in your eyes.

LOU: You know the score.

FATB: You're older.

AMY: And you won't take anymore of their shit.

Scene 19

DONNA and FATB are together. DONNA is putting on her makeup for work.

DONNA: See Bernie, what the world wants is people who can sell.

FATB: You could sell me anything.

DONNA: I know. See, it doesn't matter if you're good at school anymore. You can still make it if you're smart in a real way. In a money way.

FATB: Like you are?

DONNA: Like me. See, everyone in our year wants what I've got.

FATB: What's that?

DONNA: I'm cool!

FATB: Oh yeah.

DONNA: An that's what makes it these days. Not history, or writing reports on books. I'm getting it all ready, and then I'll get the hell out of here and down to London.

FATB: London? You can't!

DONNA: Why not? I'll take it by storm. I'll be bigger than Victoria Beckham.

FATB: You could be, you know. I can see it.

DONNA: See, I head straight down to they offices and walk in the door. An I go, 'I can't sing, I can't dance, I can't do anything. But I look like this. And I know what sells'. And they'll see a look in my eyes like I'd kill to make it. And that'll be me made.

FATB: That'd be so magic Donna.

DONNA: I won't forget you or nothing. You can be my P.A.

FATB: What's that?!

DONNA: You look after me. Get all the stuff I need.

FATB: Oh.

DONNA: We'll get to travel the world! Imagine!

FATB: The whole world!

DONNA: Ay, the whole fuckin world cryin out for us! That's what we'll have. What was that?

FATB: What?

DONNA: Is it your phone?

FATB: No, is it yours?

DONNA: Naw, mine plays FatBoy Slim now

FATB: There's no phone ringing

DONNA: Yes there is!

They listen.

DONNA: Fuck I'm going senile.

Scene 20

TESS enters. She is reading 'The Divine Invasion' by Phillip K Dick. FATB goes to her. She tries to look her in the eye. She tries to read the cover of her book. TESS moves away.

FATB: Talk to me.

TESS: What about?

FATB: About . . . stuff . . . boys . . . homework . . . whatever.

TESS: Don't start Bernie. Don't start.

FATB: What?

TESS: Don't give me that bonding shit.

FATB: Fuck sake Tess.

TESS: There's no point.

FATB: Tell me what you're reading.

TESS: You wouldn't get it.

FATB: Tell me how today was.

TESS: You'd just smile and pretend to know what I'm talking about and we'd both feel like shit. We just get on with our lives. What's it matter?

FATB: Don't talk like that.

TESS: Why not? What's wrong with the truth? Eh?

FATB: Did something happen today?

TESS: What d'you mean?

FATB: At school . . . I heard someone –

TESS: Stop talking about me behind my back.

FATB: I'm on your side here.

TESS: It was just . . . girls . . .

FATB: From your year?

TESS: From yours.

FATB: Go on.

TESS: Doesn't matter.

FATB: Tell me.

TESS: Doesn't matter.

FATB: Tell me.

TESS: I see them coming at me down the street. And right together – like they planned it – they burst out with this laugh, and its like no laugh you've ever heard. Its like . . . animals or something. And they look at me so I know its me they're after.

FATB: And then what did they do?

TESS: They . . . walked on.

FATB: Maybe they were laughing at something else.

TESS: Forget it.

FATB: Wait! I know its horrible when . . .

TESS: You know nothing about it.

FATB: Tess, wait –

TESS: What do you know about not fitting in?

FATB: Plenty.

TESS: You've got pals. All I've got is this stupid body that won't do what it should! Big breasts and no periods!

FATB: **(laughing)** Oh Tess . . . love . . .

TESS: Don't fucking laugh at me!

FATB: I'm not . . . Its just . . . everyone feels like that!

TESS: Just leave me alone! You don't get it! You don't get it at all!

Scene 21

DONNA stands in a cold blue light.

DONNA: I sneak into the boy's bogs after school. Write up all the stuff they say about me.

VOICE 1: Donna's a whoor!

VOICE 2: Donna's a tease!

VOICE 1: Donna'll suck your dick for 50p!

DONNA: Donna's easy . . .

VOICE 1: Donna's a slag!

VOICE 2: Donna's got a saggy bucket!

VOICE 1: And a face like a duck!

VOICE 2: Put a bag on her head when you do it.

DONNA: I scratch it into the tiles. Cos fuck them. Nobody's done it with you –

VOICE 1: But we know someone who has.

DONNA: I'm the sure thing.

VOICE 2: Easy.

DONNA: The Big Man initiation for every weak wee shite with a big gob and a tiny willy. They all do it. Word spreads like infection.

VOICE 1: I did it with DONNA. **(Starts repeating this over and over till end.)**

DONNA: And I say nothing! I say nothing! Cos fuck them!

Scene 22

LOU appears. She is now dressed exactly like AMY.

LOU: It was the Summer it started. I was in New Look.

AMY: Lou . . .

LOU: And I saw this gorgeous wee top.

AMY: Its not my birthday or nothing.

LOU: Its bright. Magic. But they've made it that expensive.

AMY: You shouldn't have!

LOU: But as I was walking round town it's nagging at my brain, a wee voice in my head all day. 'It's hers, you know its hers'.

AMY: Its gorgeous, Lou.

LOU: I found myself back there. Didn't know I was doing it. Happened so fast.

AMY: Why're you giving me stuff?

LOU: After that it happens again.

AMY: Shouldn't spend all your money.

LOU: I got good, bringing stuff to get the tags off. I did it in shops where the girls at school worked.

AMY: Its lovely.

LOU: They gabbed away to me before I did it.

AMY: Really lovely.

LOU: And they didn't know. Best buzz in the world.

AMY: What are you like?!

LOU: Next to giving it to Amy. . .

AMY: Lou . . .

LOU: Next to seeing her smile.

Scene 23

TESS is alone.

TESS: All you have . . . all the time . . . is opening your mouth and having folk stare at you. Like you're speaking some language they'll never understand. And its like you've lived your whole life in some alternative universe, and been eating different food, and hearing different sounds, and watching different television. All they do is look at you with –

VOICE 1: Freak.

TESS: In their eyes. And they're scared cos they can't put you in any fuckin box no matter how they try. It makes them short circuit or something. And every day, every single day you've got a big hole inside you and you don't know what the hell it means. And then one day in some stupid corny film or some stupid TV programme some stupid character says –

VOICE 1: I'm lonely.

TESS: And you almost fall apart right there, because that's what it is, how you feel and you never even knew. You're alone. You're alone. You're so fucking alone and you can't bear it anymore. And then one day it happens for you, some wisecracking teacher who's trying to relate, lets you on a computer and its all you ever wanted to see. And it all makes sense. And finally! Finally! It's something that works the way your mind works! And it's the sound of a million doors opening, and you don't have to be stuck in your pissy wee room in a pissy wee city. You can scream through the doors into space! And maybe, if you're lucky, some other freak'll call back at you .Cos everyone needs to feel at home sometimes. And not alone.

DONNA, LOU and AMY together. AMY is picking up LOU and swinging her round.

DONNA: Hey, did you hear?

LOU: What?

DONNA: FatB against the hospital wall. Guess who with?

AMY: Wee freaky Pete?

DONNA: Nup.

AMY: Who then?

DONNA: Nobody we know!

LOU: You're kidding!

DONNA: I'm not!

AMY: Naebody we know!

LOU: You're kidding!

DONNA: I'm not!

AMY: Naebody we know! How does she know naebody we know?

DONNA: I'm telling you the truth!

AMY: Tongues n all?

DONNA: Tongues n not caring who's watching.

LOU: Nice kissing or what?

DONNA: What d'you mean?

LOU: Was it like. . . *Titanic* . . . or was it like *Trainspotting*?

DONNA: Dunno.

AMY: Was he slobbering on her?

DONNA: She didn't seem to mind.

AMY: Way to go FatB!

LOU: Ay, who'd have thought it!

AMY: She's no that fat I s'pose.

DONNA: She is.

AMY: No, she's not Britney, but she's not . . .

DONNA: No she is. Well, come on! She is.

Lights focus on FATB.

FATB: Mum always sent me to a pharmacy across town. Don't want folk knowing all our business she said. 'Don't want that lemon-faced cow round the corner knowing all our ins and outs'. Now I go all the way over there just to see him . . . Martin. In his sparkling white coat. His smile's sexy as hell. We gab away like anything. I feel like . . . I'm safe . . . like . . . I'm home. And its not that way where your voice disappears down your throat and you squeak like Minnie mouse or something! I'm funny. And he's funny. And we're the same kind of funny. And it's like . . . all over my body . . . every single particle of me is alive or something! All of my skin and all of my hair and all of my arms and legs and fingers and toes are just waiting for him to touch me! And if he does I might explode! I might just explode! Cos if he does touch me, if I'm too busy gabbing to notice a car and I'm about to die or something, he'll pull me back and laugh and it's the best thing in the world! The best bloody thing in the world!

Scene 24

FATB: It was a bright Summer. A brilliant Summer. A never wanting to head home Summer.

AMY: A wondering if you could still sulk –

DONNA: Still strut

FATB: Still strike a pose Summer. **(Beat)** It was a sad Summer.

AMY: Like getting old.

FATB: There'd be laughs –

DONNA: Loads of laughs to come –

AMY: But different.

FATB: We'd become –

AMY: Something –

LOU: Gone our separate ways –

DONNA: And strange –

LOU: There was no reachin back into the past for it –

AMY: No searching for something that's vanished –

DONNA: Over the curve of the road –

LOU: Our old selves –

AMY: Smashed wi the glass bottles in the wee kid's playpark.

LOU: And nothing to be the same again –

DONNA: Whatever they say –

LOU: Nothing.

For a second they burst into the pop video dance routine of the start, but this time the sound and movement is distorted and fragmented. They cannot seem to get into stride and the music fades out.

Scene 25

AMY appears, she is crashing round the space, climbing and kicking at things, trying to burn off the frustration inside her.

LOU: Amy, wait, please . . .

AMY: What is it?

LOU: Tell me what happened.

AMY: I just –

LOU: What?

AMY: Got in a fight.

LOU: Amy!

AMY: I knew you'd say that!

LOU: How?

AMY: What's your problem? So I took him out. I was tryin to run the track, and he keeps starin at me!

LOU: Staring?

AMY: Yes! His eyes all over me! And laughing. Couldn't block him out.

LOU: But people are always laughing at us. What's it matter?

AMY: Why aren't you proud of me?

LOU: I don't like fighting.

AMY: You can't let people walk all over you, Lou! I couldn't let them think I was weak.

LOU: Never that eh?

AMY: I pushed his face first, and he's still laughing at me. So I slapped him across the face. And that gives him a fright. Looks at me and sees I mean it. An he's fighting with himself cos he's not supposed to fight girls and all. And then I piss him off and he starts fighting back. And everyone's looking and it gets my blood up and I'm not gonna be beat and I keep on and on and he keeps on and on, and we're rolling around with grit in our eyes and he can't take it! So he goes for my tits, punching hard, so I knee him in the balls and then he's finished. I leave him then, I don't keep at him when he's down.

LOU: Right.

AMY: An then it's like nothing else I've known. Walkin through that crowd. With them all starin. An some of them hate you. But some of them love you. An some of them can't believe what they've seen.

LOU: What're they gonna do to you?

AMY: Don't know yet. I told them I did it. They can't take it. Old Fife's convinced I must be innocent cos I'm a girl, and Old Green thinks I should get it worse cos I'm a girl.

LOU: Why'd you do it?

AMY: Cos he was laughing

LOU: But he's not worth it.

AMY: You weren't there. You know nothing about it.

LOU: If it was some guy slapping girls about you'd be onto him in a shot.

AMY: You weren't there!

LOU: You need something to give you a story. That's what you need.

AMY: Is it? Or is it what you need.

LOU: I can't watch you knocking chunks out of people –

AMY: Fine.

LOU: They'll be after you.

AMY: At the bell I'm out the side door! They won't even see me for dust!

LOU: They'll get you eventually

AMY: What d'you want me to do Lou? Take whatever they throw at me lying down.

LOU: Sometimes you've got to learn to walk away.

AMY: Like you do.

AMY leaves. The Dead Girl appears. She looks LOU in the eye. LOU tries to reach out and touch her. The Dead Girl remains cold, impassive. The Dead Girl leaves.

Scene 26

DONNA is alone. There is a cold white light on her, an unforgiving spotlight this time.

DONNA: The Summer I gave up fighting them. You figure you might as well be what they call you. And you just get too tired to keep saying no. First time you do it you feel good for a bit. But it was an awkward an a lonely thing. An you couldnae even look each other in the eye after. So you figure it's you, and maybe you're –

VOICE 2: Tight.

VOICE 1: Frigid.

DONNA: Crap at it or something. I wish there was a way of waiting without them dumping you.

VOICE 1: Once a guy's started . . .

DONNA: Cos I remember how it used to be, when he could only hold you and kiss you and that. It was kind of sweet. Sometimes I wonder if they want to go back too. Boys. I just . . . that's what I think sometimes. That's all.

The Dead Girl passes through.

Scene 27

FATB: He looks at me. Martin. My heart's fit to burst right out me. He says:
'I was just – well I thought . . . .'
An I say: 'Yeah . . . '

He says: 'I just . . .' **(Laughs)** 'Probably not but . . .'
'What?'
'Silly but – probably – thought – if you – its a – Saturday.
Are you . . . ? Anything. . . ? Well maybe you – probably don't but – maybe – it's a – I thought . . . .'
Then I let him off the hook.
'So Saturday?'
'Just – a film – or – a – eight?'
'Eight?'
That's thrown him.
'Or seven? Or nine? Or . . . .'
'Eight's good.'
'Good!'
'See you,' we say.
'See you.'
'See you.'
'See you.'

Scene 28

AMY: Standin by the scaffoldin, the old hospital wall –

DONNA: Darin Amy to climb it, silent, darin with our eyes.

LOU: But no –

DONNA: But no –

FATB: She stays on the ground.

AMY: Canna be arsed

DONNA: N mebbe its a kids thing. Like playparks and paggers –

AMY: Mebbe its no excitin –

LOU: Just stopped climbing maybe –

AMY: You ken what you'll see.

FATB: You ken what the view is.

DONNA: You ken what the score is.

AMY: Nae fuckin point.

FATB: Standin by the scaffoldin, the old hospital wall –

LOU: Its gonna go any day now –

DONNA: Blow it up –

AMY: Pull it down.

LOU: They've got to keep the front of it. Its old, see? Protected.

FATB: Just the sad wee front, standin on its own.

DONNA: Fake front of a wall, wi nothin behind –

AMY: Standin brave an cocky like, with the windows all holes –

DONNA: We'll be there to see it go –

AMY: We'll be cheerin as they do it –

LOU: We'll be there to see it go.

FATB: Come crumbling down round us.

Scene 29

TESS: One day when they wake up I'll be gone. No more voices behind your back.

VOICE 1: Freak.

VOICE 2: Loser.

TESS: I'll show them. I'll laugh in their face. I met him online. He's called Mark. He has the mark of the chosen one. Says I have to meet him. We'll understand each other. I read his mind down the computer. I just want to talk to someone. Without seeing.

VOICE 2: Freak.

TESS: In their eyes. I try. But its so tiring . . . trying to be yourself. All this is . . . is . . .

VOICE 1: Game one.

TESS: All this we think is real. There's a battle between the two worlds. I know it! There's a message in the frequency between radio stations, a picture forming in the static. It's the other world fighting to get through.

VOICE 2: Freak.

TESS: They're waiting for someone like me.

VOICE 1: Loser.

TESS: Who's not just nose down living. Who can look up and see the sky. Its not just who you hang with. You're getting scarred. And however they mark you, you'll keep chasing to change it your whole life. The cool ones want to be clever. The smart ones want to be liked. The freaks just want to fit in. Branded all the time – thirteen, sixteen, eighteen, forever. Its all initiation. They just never call it that.

Scene 30

LOU and FATB are together. DONNA and AMY appear. They are shoving at each other.

DONNA: **(To LOU)** Just fucking admit it. **(To AMY)** You want a kickin?

AMY: From you?

DONNA: Ay

AMY: Don't make me laugh

DONNA: Don't know what you think you are these days –

AMY: Get out my face Donna –

DONNA: Strutting about like you think you're something. An as fur her! **(Turns on LOU.)**

AMY: You say nothing about her! You hear me?

DONNA: Just fuckin get out of here!

AMY: Fuck you!

LOU: Calm the fucks eh?

AMY/DONNA: Keep out of it!

LOU: Hey . . . !

DONNA: I saw you do it! In my shop, ya cow!

LOU: Do what?

DONNA: I saw you take it!

LOU: Don't know what you're talking about.

AMY: You just leave her alone!

DONNA: Or what? Any fuckin shop but mine, all right?

AMY: Lou'd never do it!

DONNA: You keep out of it!

AMY: You worry about your own life – an keepin your legs and gob shut once in a while!

DONNA throws herself at AMY who pushes her off.

AMY: I'll not touch you, all right? Just get away from me!

DONNA: You two better sort it. You're over the edge.

AMY: Oh fuck you!

DONNA: Fuck you!

AMY: Fuck you!

FATB pulls DONNA away from them, they exit.

AMY: What's she on, eh?

LOU: I don't know.

Pause.

AMY: Guess what?

LOU: What?

AMY: The best thing!

LOU: Tell me.

AMY: Today wee Spud comes up looking shit scared and says there's gonna be a kickabout after school! An God – they never ask us to play right?

LOU: You can't, Amy.

AMY: Why not?

LOU: Why d'you think they asked you?

AMY: They think I can play! I don't play like a girl or nothing.

LOU: You're getting to them.

AMY: Don't know what you mean.

LOU: They want to get you back for battering Souser.

AMY: No!

LOU: You think they'll let you get away with it?

AMY: Stop being paranoid.

LOU: I'm just saying –

AMY: It's all forgotten.

LOU: You'd be stupid to go.

AMY: You're so scared of the world, you know that? You've got to fuckin live!

LOU: Stop swearing at me!

AMY: You can't be afraid of boys. They smell the fear on you. You've got to fling yourself out across the mud with them. Get the ball before anyone!

LOU: So it's to prove something?

AMY: The whole school'll be watching!

LOU: Not the whole school.

AMY: Pretty much. You're just jealous.

LOU: I'm worried about you.

AMY: Don't bother.

AMY leaves and LOU follows her.

Scene 31

FATB: What was that about?

DONNA: She gets on my tits.

FATB: Amy?

DONNA: Both of them. Something's got to change, B, we've got to blow this open.

FATB: Blow what open?

DONNA: It can't go on, you ken that? Like we're lassies and what we do means nothin.

FATB: Why're you so ragin?

DONNA: Her. Lou. Her kind. Should keep her hands to herself.

FATB: Her kind?

DONNA: You ken what I mean.

FATB: What's going on,eh? This is us. Strong. The girls.

DONNA: What the fuck does that mean anymore? All you've got is what you can grab wi both hands and hold onto. An fuckin Princess Lou's out to pull it all apart for us. Tryin to get us sacked. Choryin stuff she doesn't even want to make out she's no as fucking dull as she seems.

FATB: What's this about?

DONNA: It's about everything.

Pause.

DONNA: We'll just make it you an me this weekend. Fuck them.

FATB: I'm . . . busy.

DONNA: What?

FATB: It's always youse fuckin out your faces knowin I'll get youse home!

DONNA: What're you talkin about?

FATB: I've got a date's what.

DONNA: I've seen you with him

FATB: What?

DONNA: Doesnae seem like much

FATB: What?!

DONNA: Forget it B, an come out with us!

FATB: All I get is worryin. Cookin and cleanin and makin sure my Da's comfy or my sister's fed. Makin sure he's taken his medicine and not thrown it up or thrown it away. An when I do go out all I get is looking after you.

DONNA: Nobody makes you.

FATB: If I don't do it no one does.

DONNA: We're sorry about your Da an all . . .

FATB: Things do have to change. You're right.

DONNA: Is that what your new boyfriend says?

FATB: It's what I say.

DONNA: Yeah. An where you gonna be without us eh? Tell me that.

DONNA leaves.

Scene 32

AMY, LOU, FATB and DONNA are together.

AMY: We're all there when it goes –

DONNA: Blows –

FATB: Comes crashing down –

DONNA: We cheer as they do it.

LOU: Though they're taking something from us –

AMY: Old hospital wall.

DONNA: Scene of so many snogs with greasy chip fingers –

AMY: Scene of so many fights –

LOU: Floor scattered wi condoms and battered old syringes –

DONNA: Scene of so many double dates –

LOU: And emergency briefings –

FATB: What should I do?

DONNA: He loves us, loves us not. He loves us, loves us not.

AMY: Scene of too many crimes, but its done now –

FATB: Gone now.

DONNA: Fuck it.

LOU: Old hospital wall –

FATB: An naebody asked us!

LOU: They'd never ask us.

DONNA: No they'd never ask us.

AMY: Naw they'd never.

Scene 33

FATB, LOU and AMY.

FATB: Did you hear?

AMY: What?

FATB: Donna.

AMY: What about her?

FATB: Got herself . . . pregnant.

AMY: You what?

FATB: She has! She is! I heard!

AMY: Bollocks.

FATB: It's the truth.

LOU: She told you?

FATB: Well she willnae will she?

AMY: Shoots her mouth off about other folk enough.

LOU: What'll we say to her?

AMY: We canny say nothing to her.

FATB: Why?

AMY: She's got to tell us herself.

LOU: This is stupid.

FATB: She won't want folk talking about her.

LOU: But we are talking about her!

FATB: We're different! We're her friends!

AMY: Well . . . she had it comin maybe.

FATB: What?

AMY: It's what you're thinking

LOU: Amy . . .

FATB: You just leave her alone!

FATB leaves them.

LOU: What's got into you?

AMY: Nothing.

LOU: You never used to be so hard on folk. An you used to talk to me. I feel like . . . I'm losing you.

AMY: You know what you sound like?

LOU: Its like we're not . . .

AMY: Drop it.

LOU: All that stuff I give you. Donna was right. I take it. So we can be close again. Don't you see?

AMY: You'd never steal nothing.

LOU: I do. So I can give you things.

AMY: What, you think I want that junk?

LOU: Don't –

AMY: Never heard anythin so stupid –

LOU: I went in the police station! And they looked at me like I was a nice girl, brought up right. And then I told them what I'd done. I really got them!

AMY: You got no one! Its fuckin sad that's what it is! Take what you want but don't try and blame me for it. Its not cool or flatterin or nothin, its creepy, that's all.

LOU: Don't say that, I'm warning you!

AMY: Or what? . . . You'll copy me to death? **(Laughs.)**

LOU: Please Amy. Its always been you and me.

AMY: You're a fuckin loser you know that? A loser.

Scene 34

TESS is alone. FATB joins her.

FATB: You all right? Tess?

TESS: What d'you think?

FATB: I don't know. What you been doing?

TESS: Nothing you'd understand.

FATB: Try me.

TESS: Just drop it Bernie.

FATB: Why can't we talk?

TESS: You tell me.

FATB: I'm tryin Tess . . .

TESS: God yeah. Mother Teresa B. Everyone knows you try . . .

FATB: It's not like that.

TESS: What is it like then? You never let me do anything in the house – like you're sure I'd mess it up. You never let me talk to him – not that there's any point. Someone should have stopped them havin us – they were too old!

FATB: They were always there for us

TESS: Mum died!

FATB: I know.

TESS: An Dad hardly knows we're there.

FATB: That's not true. Come on eh? There's you and me, that's something.

TESS: Stop tryin to pretend we've got something strong. That we're family. We're nothing. A bunch of losers clinging together, a fat girl, a freak and a vegetable!

FATB slaps TESS.

FATB: Don't you ever say that! Not till you've carried him from the bed to the loo and he gives you a look like he knows what's going on and hates the whole humiliation of it! All he wants in the world is to be himself again! D'you not remember him swinging us round and round as kids? And coming out with some stupid Monty Python line at the wrong moment? And playing bloody Bob Dylan! An his magic cooking! He's still all that! He is!

TESS: He's dead now Bernie. As good as. He doesn't know we're here.

FATB: Get away from me. Go. I don't want to see you.

Scene 35

DONNA: I eat something funny. And I'm throwing up in the bogs. And when I come out, looking rough as fuck, I see that cow Sally Byatt looking at me. An she gives me one of her smiles, like she's ready to spit out glass at you the next minute. An I know she's thought of some way to get me. And its not cos she's worth anythin. But to have someone stand there hatin you like that. To know you're hated. Anyhow. That's when it starts. And its just a laugh at first. I mean –

VOICE 1: Slag!

DONNA: I reckon folk who know me'll know –

VOICE 2: Slag's knocked up!

DONNA: They'll listen –

VOICE 1: Got what she deserves!

DONNA: An we'll go laugh in Byatt's face –

VOICE 2: Up the fucking duff!

DONNA: We'll stand there tough as rock –

VOICE 2: Stupit cow!

DONNA: And watch her crumble, I'll say nothing –

BOTH VOICES: Stupit fuckin bitch!

DONNA: And the true folk'll show themselves –

VOICE 1: She had it coming!

DONNA: They'll be there. They'll be there. They will.

Scene 36

AMY: Things break up. Its how life is. People hold you back is all. When they talk about ties . . . I never wanted them. Never wanted the shitty Girl Guides. Never wanted to join. Lou goes on like she's lost the whole world. We were just a gang is all. Not like cool, or New York or nothing. Just girls who got stuck together, who hung about. Canny even remember how it started. People crash into each other is all. Doesn't make you who you are. Lou says a lot of things. But what does she know?

Scene 37

TESS: How old are you?

VOICE 1: How old do you think I am?

TESS: Nineteen?

VOICE 1: Age is a state of mind!

TESS: Yeah. I think that too.

VOICE 1: Tell me what you like to do.

TESS: What do you mean?

VOICE 1: Tell me what you wear to school.

TESS: Why?

VOICE 1: You feel lonely sometimes?

TESS: Do you?

VOICE 1: I guess everyone does.

TESS: That's true.

VOICE 1: You know we should meet.

TESS: You think?

VOICE 1: Definitely. I feel close to you.

TESS: Really?

VOICE 1: Will you meet me?

TESS: Is that what you want?

VOICE 1: Yes. If you're in this for real. Are you in this for real?

TESS: Yes.

Scene 38

FATB: Talk to me Donna.

DONNA: Why? What did Amy say?

FATB: We didn't know what to say.

DONNA: But you believed it. Don't bother. She as good as said it to my face. Count on old Amy for that.

FATB: I'll help you Donna. It was a shock but –

DONNA: I don't need your help.

FATB: Please . . .

DONNA: I'm not pregnant.

FATB: What?

DONNA: Never thought of that, eh?

FATB: But you never said . . .

DONNA: What was the point? People believe what they want.

FATB: I'm sorry.

DONNA: Sorry gets you nowhere. Bernie, I thought you'd put two fingers up to the world! I thought you'd be the one who knew.

FATB: I do. I am.

DONNA: I slept with one guy. Once. And that was only cos of what folk called me.

FATB: You lied to me.

DONNA: You believed it.

Scene 39

AMY: It all went to fuck that Summer.

LOU: A messed up Summer.

AMY: A ripped out and torn up Summer.

LOU: A not wanting to be what we were Summer.

DONNA: Looking at ourselves in the mirror –

FATB: Hating the look of your face.

AMY: It was a fucked up Summer.

DONNA: With losers and losing.

LOU: See us at the corner.

AMY: See us coming at you.

FATB: And you'd see right through us.

AMY: It was a gone to fuck Summer.

LOU: Pushed apart when we could have done something.

FATB: It was the Summer I lost Tess. My fault. Wasn't watching.

Scene 40

DONNA: She's this weird wee thing – admit it! Everyone thinks it but no one'll say it! She was just Bernie's weird wee sister who hung about us cos there was no one else!

LOU: How can you say that now?

DONNA: None of us could handle her! So don't go pretending you were her best friend or nothing now!

LOU: She wasn't weird.

AMY: You couldn't talk to her!

LOU: She was clever.

DONNA: She was weird!

FATB appears.

FATB: Is that what you think?

LOU: Shit.

DONNA: I'm just saying!

FATB: Just shut it!

LOU: We should have talked to her more –

DONNA: What was there to say?

LOU: She'll come back B,

DONNA: She might be in trouble, B.

FATB: Thanks Donna.

DONNA: What do you want me to say?

FATB: You don't give a fuck about anyone do you? Unless its anyone you can fuck. Why is no one doing anything? It should be in every paper, it should – tell me the last thing you said to her.

AMY: I don't remember.

FATB: You do.

AMY: We talked about – fighting – telling the truth.

FATB: And what do you know about truth? Tell me she's got some friend we never knew about! Feeding her and keeping her safe. Tell me she'll come back and I can just hug her and hug her and never let her go! Tell me that! Tell me! **(To LOU)** You tell me what to do! You're supposed to be so smart.

LOU: I don't know.

FATB: Its not enough! She's not skinny-build-blonde, hair-dark, jacket-jeans – she's – she's – ! You can't watch everyone all the time! You can't hold together all the cracks! Its too much! Too much! Too much!

Scene 41

AMY: Best game of footie. Half the school there. Lou was there, like the old Lou, screaming for me. And I'm quick and I'm sleek. I'm a star out there and everyone can see it.

LOU: And then there's a moment, like its all been planned –

AMY: Someone's foot catches me, and I'm down –

LOU: And when she's down, they all surround her.

AMY: And the game stops.

LOU: And the crowd holds its breath.

AMY: And I look up at their faces, and I see they mean it. And the wee guy I did over is standing at the back.

LOU: And I can't breathe and I can't move –

AMY: And its leather and mud and boots and studs –

LOU: And I look around and the crowd's all frozen –

AMY: And the breath's knocked out of me –

LOU: And there are faces that cheer it on, and faces that just let it happen –

AMY: And they're at my ribs, my back, a million feet, legs, at me –

LOU: And I can't hear a sound but my breathing –

AMY: I can't breathe for the blood –

LOU: And I'm scrabbling through air to get at her and all I can do is watch –

AMY: And the wee guy gets revenge.

LOU: And everyone who feared her lay right into her –

AMY: And just as the world is spinning and almost turned black, it stops. And there's nothing.

LOU: They drop me in the mud.

AMY: And all I can hear is the silence of the pitch, and the wind, and Lou sobbing, sobbing, sobbing above me. They've taken the wind out of me.

Scene 42

LOU: They used to see us at the corner –

AMY: See us coming at them.

DONNA: And you'd see them stand back.

FATB: And you'd see them take cover.

AMY: Cos we were strong.

DONNA: Cos we were something. We could wipe them out with a look.

AMY: Slice through them –

DONNA: With a sneer or something –

FATB: But it was such a fucked Summer –

DONNA: I never knew what happened.

FATB: One minute we were there –

DONNA: Me and FatB

LOU: Amy and Lou.

FATB: And Tess –

LOU: Tess –

DONNA: Tess –

AMY: Tess –

FATB: And the next we'd exploded.

LOU: Feels like –

DONNA: Feels like –

FATB: Feels like –

AMY: But you just keep going –

FATB: And any minute – any minute now, Tess'll walk in the door and we'll be complete again . . . We will . . . We will . . . We will . . .

AMY: You go in the ring you've got to take a few blows.

Scene 43

AMY is still beaten up and bruised.

AMY: I scared them see? So that was something. I was so good they had to take me out. One day I'll run and run so fast I'll leave you all behind. I'll be shining on the telly, a streak of lightning flashing through the Olympics, picking up all the gold. And Dunny and Johnson and all they boys who laugh at girls'll have nothing to say . . . they'll have nothing to say.

Pause. The lights focus on LOU.

LOU: It was the Summer we lost it. And Tess went missing. And a dead girl got dumped on the beach. And there were all these voices, calling us names, all Summer. And some of the names stuck. Mouthy, Quiet, Fat, Slag, Freak. Sometimes without your mates you think you might just spin off empty into space. They say it means nothing, who you hang with. But sometimes its your anchor. Sometimes its all you've got. We were all there that Summer. And the next we were gone.

End

Other plays published by Capercaillie Books

Oedipus The Visionary by David Greig

ISBN 0-9549625-1-6

Electra by Tom McGrath

ISBN 0-9549625-2-4

Opium Eater by Andrew Dallmeyer

ISBN 0-9549625-3-2

The Salt Wound by Stephen Greenhorn

ISBN 0-9549625-0-8

Dissent by Stephen Greenhorn

ISBN 0-9545206-9-6

£8.99

Available from Booksource

Tel: +44(0)8702 402 182 Fax: +44(0)1415 570 189

email: customerservices@booksource.net

Web orders at www.capercailliebooks.co.uk